DREAM. INSPIRE. CREATE.

VISIT US ONLINE:
www.YoungDreamersPress.com

TAG US IN YOUR PHOTOS & VIDEOS:
www.instagram.com/youngdreamerspress
www.tiktok.com/@youngdreamerspress

WE'RE ALSO ON FACEBOOK:
www.facebook.com/youngdreamerspress

©2019 YOUNG DREAMERS PRESS
ALL RIGHTS RESERVED.

NO PART OF THIS PUBLICATION MAY BE REPRODUCED, DISTRIBUTED, OR TRANSMITTED IN ANY FORM OR BY ANY MEANS INCLUDING PHOTOCOPYING, RECORDING, OR OTHER ELECTRONIC OR MECHANICAL METHODS, WITHOUT THE PRIOR WRITTEN PERMISSION OF THE PUBLISHER, EXCEPT IN THE CASE OF BRIEF QUOTATIONS EMBODIED IN CRITICAL REVIEWS AND CERTAIN OTHER NON-COMMERCIAL USES PERMITTED BY COPYRIGHT LAW.

www.ingramcontent.com/pod-product-compliance
Lightning Source LLC
Chambersburg PA
CBHW081102070526
44583CB00019B/2518